THE SH!T IN THE MIDDLE

THE SH!T IN THE MIDDLE

HOW TO FIX YOUR OPERATIONS, INCREASE PROFIT, AND STOP FLYING BLIND

JASON STOCKTON

THE SH!T IN THE MIDDLE: HOW TO FIX YOUR OPERATIONS, INCREASE PROFIT, AND STOP FLYING BLIND

Credits:
Copy Editor: Tina Morganella
Book Design & Layout: Karolina Kruk-Umięcka

Published by: Jason Stockton, Melbourne, Australia

First Edition
ISBN: 978-1-7646065-0-9 (Paperback)
ISBN: 978-1-7646065-1-6 (Ebook)

PREFACE

Over the years, I've made a lot of mistakes in business.

I've built and sold small businesses, worked inside global brands like PUMA, and eventually founded Supply'd ERP, an operational enterprise resource planning (ERP) for food and retail businesses. I've seen what works at scale, and I've learned the hard way what doesn't.

I left PUMA, where I'd just grown their ecommerce business massively in Australia and New Zealand, to start a chocolate business with my wife. We made incredible products. Handcrafted, and arguably some of the best chocolate in the world. We had customers who loved us. We had revenue.

And yet, we barely broke even.

For years, I couldn't figure out why. We had a great product. We had sales. We were operationally efficient, churning out considerable volumes with just one or two chocolatiers. So why weren't we profitable?

It wasn't because we executed poorly. It was because I didn't do the hard economic work early enough. I didn't truly understand which products, prices, volumes, and channels could ever produce meaningful profit. The strategy was built on assumptions, not facts. The boat was sailing. Smoothly. Efficiently. Just in the wrong direction – straight into a storm.

Most business books talk about revenue and marketing. That's important – you do need solid revenue to have a good business. What they won't tell you is that 60% of businesses fail in the first 5 years, and of those that survive, almost half never make a profit. They're generating revenue while burning cash through inefficient operations, poor margin management, and unoptimised processes.

That's what this book is about – the stuff between your revenue and your profit. This is the sh!t in the middle that actually determines whether your business survives.

I eventually sold the chocolate business to focus on Supply'd. Since then, I've worked with numerous businesses facing the same problems I faced. This book is everything I wish I'd known before I started.

I'm going to skip the fluff and get straight to the point. You'll get the frameworks, the formulas, and the honest lessons from where I went wrong – so you don't have to.

Now, let's explore the sh!t in the middle.

CONTENTS

CHAPTER 1

WHAT IS THE SH!T IN THE MIDDLE?

Most business books out there talk about the top line (aka revenue). As a result, most business owners and managers focus on growth and don't necessarily consider whether the growth is profitable or not. There are many businesses that have tens of millions in revenue, but their bottom line (aka profit) is slimmer than a gluten-free pancake.

While top line growth is important, most of us get into business for the profit. The sh!t in the middle of the profit and loss (P&L) often grows at the same rate (or sometimes at a higher rate) than the top line, meaning it doesn't matter how much you turn over, you cannot reach profitability. Having revenue of ten million dollars without profit is just vanity. Having a healthy bottom line is good business.

In this book, we're going to focus on the sh!t in the middle. If you can master this, you can increase profitability dramatically without needing to add to the top line. Once you do grow the top line, your expenses will grow at a slower rate, and your profitability grows with it.

THE ANATOMY OF A P&L

Before we go any further, we first need to understand how to read a P&L. If you're experienced with P&Ls you're welcome to skip ahead to the next chapter.

The P&L is not just something your accountant uses to understand the health of your business. It's also how *you* know whether the business is profitable or not. If you have to wait for your next accountant meeting to see this and understand it, you're already on the back foot.

The P&L is usually presented as net sales and expense amounts (any amount exclusive of taxes). By excluding tax from both your sales and purchases, you avoid factoring amounts that will be paid to the tax department.

To help you out, here are the key components of the P&L:

PROFIT & LOSS STATEMENT

REVENUE / SALES	$1,000,000	← TOP LINE
COST OF GOODS SOLD	($400,000)	← COST OF GOODS SOLD
OPERATING EXPENSES:		
Rent	($50,000)	
Salaries	($200,000)	← EXPENSES
Utilities	($20,000)	
Marketing	($30,000)	
NET INCOME / (LOSS)	$300,000	← BOTTOM LINE

TOP LINE

The top line is revenue and sales coming into the business. While we're not going to be focused on the top line in this book, it is important you have a healthy top line to have a good business.

COST OF GOODS SOLD

Your cost of goods sold (COGS) is exactly what it says it is on the tin. It is the cost of any goods you have sold to date. Many businesses allocate all their purchases to the COGS, but while this is okay at the start, it is not technically correct. You should only allocate the COGS once the item has been actually sold. The amount allocated should be the landed cost with all the freight fees, and any other costs related to getting the product to you included in it. Or, if you produce it in house, inclusive of all components and labour. We'll go into more detail on this later in the book.

EXPENSES

Expenses include any costs of operating the business. This can also be referred to as operating expenses (OPEX), or outgoings. It is easy to look at these numbers but it is much harder to analyse and understand what sits behind them. You aren't going to save your business by cutting out the small expenses. Don't worry, though, we're going to deep dive into this in a lot of detail.

BOTTOM LINE

The bottom line is your net profit. For small businesses this is pretty straightforward. It is what money has been earned by the business for the given period. Unfortunately, this is not free cash though. Often, it is tied up in inventory or other business expenses for the next month. As your business gets larger, this line typically becomes EBIT (earnings before interest and tax), EBI-

TA (earnings before interest, tax, and amortisation) or EBITDA (earnings before interest, tax, depreciation, and amortisation). These are all slightly different variations of how much money your core business actually made from trading before the bank takes its interest and the tax department takes their cut, or in some cases before depreciation and amortisation is factored in.

THE SH!T IN THE MIDDLE

When we refer to the sh!t in the middle, we are referring to everything between the top line and bottom line, specifically your COGS and expenses. Ensuring this remains healthy is not as simple as cutting a few costs here and there. You need to take a step back and look at the big picture. We'll deep dive into this throughout this book, starting with understanding your true margins.

CHAPTER REVISION

Check your understanding of the chapter topic by answering the following questions:

- What is your top line?
- What is your bottom line?
- What are your COGS?
- What are your expenses?
- What is the sh!t in the middle?

CHAPTER 2

WHY YOUR MARGINS ARE LYING TO YOU: UNDERSTANDING YOUR TRUE MARGIN

Before you do anything in the business, you need to understand your TRUE margins. I'm not talking about the estimated costs you were working on 12 months ago – I'm talking about a live margin, including all relevant costs.

Getting your margins wrong can have a negative impact on your business. I have firsthand experience of getting this wrong. With our chocolate business, we had two key products: hand-crafted bonbons and, of course, chocolate bars. The chocolate bars were easy to make, whereas the bonbons were so labour-intensive we felt like they were not scalable. So, naturally, I heavily marketed the chocolate bars. There was a big problem though. The chocolate bars didn't sell as well as the bonbons. The bonbons outsold the chocolate bars by a long way, no matter what I did. In hindsight, it's easy to see why – they had a clear unique selling point. Chocolate bars are in every store, bonbons are not.

Once we began tracking the costs of each batch, including the actual labour involved, it became clear that the bonbons actually had an 85% margin at retail. Our best-selling product had an amazing margin. Yet, I was pushing chocolate bars, which were a harder sell, that only had a 60% margin, and no real unique selling point. If I had done the right work earlier, I would have made a better decision and could have invested in automation to solve the scalability problem. This is why accurate, live margins, including labour, are mission-critical. Every decision you make in the business should be guided by them. Be sure to track every batch. Your gut feeling about which products are profitable is probably wrong.

There are two ways to calculate your margin: accounting and operational. Let's explore them in a little more detail.

ACCOUNTING MARGIN

The accounting margin considers all costs in the business, including goods, labour and all other overheads, to work out your true margin. This is difficult to calculate upfront and maintain because it requires final P&L costings; it is otherwise terribly inaccurate and can lead you to overprice or underprice your product.

Typically, the accounting margin is best left to your P&L rather than trying to distribute not yet finalised business costs down to a product level. Instead, make sure you have sufficient margin to cover all your costs, keeping in mind that volume is a critical factor, which we will talk about later on.

OPERATIONAL MARGIN

The second and more common way to calculate your margin is operational. This is the margin we'll be working with in this book. The operational margin considers any operational expenses related to the manufacture of the product. This would include the cost of any goods, labour and inbound freight.

If your products are manufactured by a third party, this is easy – it's simply calculated by using the landed cost of the product. This would be what you paid for the product, plus any shipping costs or duties paid to get the product to your warehouse.

The percentage you have for the operational margin needs to cover your overheads with enough left over for profit. To calculate our operational margin, we first need to establish our landed cost. There are a number of different methods to calculate your landed cost for an item.

Freight by unit cost

To calculate your freight by unit cost, for each item on the order, divide the net unit cost by the net total of the order and times it by the net freight amount. If you add this to the unit cost, you will get your landed cost.

$$LandedCost = UnitCost + (\frac{UnitCost}{NetOrderTotal} * NetFreight)$$

Freight by unit quantity

To calculate your freight by quantity, you must first know your total unit count on the order. Divide the net freight amount by the total number of units, then add this to your unit cost to get your landed cost.

$$LandedCost = UnitCost + \frac{NetFreight}{TotalUnits}$$

Freight by unit cubic weight

To calculate your freight by cubic weight (volumetric size), for each item on the order, divide the unit cubic weight by the total cubic weight of the order and times it by the net freight amount. Add this to the unit cost, to get your landed cost.

$$LandedCost = UnitCost + (\frac{UnitCubicWeight}{OrderCubicWeight} * NetFreight)$$

Personally, I use the freight by item cost as my preferred way to consider the final cost, but any method is fine. If you have additional costs, such as credit card fees or handling charges, add this to the total freight cost before doing the formulas above to factor it in. If you are drop-shipping, it would simply be what you paid for the item itself; you do not consider any outbound freight, only inbound.

If you manufacture the product in house, it is a bit harder to calculate. You need to factor in the landed cost of each ingredient or component, labour costs, wastage and yields. The challenge here is that the ingredient or component costs often vary, particularly once you factor in freight. Labour costs vary almost every run and yields can be unpredictable. The ultimate way to track all of this is using a manufacturing-based ERP or inventory software like Supply'd ERP. These often have powerful tools to calculate real landed costs, track labour on every production run and determine real yields. This would mean every run has an accurate margin to work with, based on the specific batches and lots used and other variable factors.

If you're just starting out, however, you might not be able to justify the investment in an ERP or inventory software. In this case, you will need to use a spreadsheet to track your runs.

Even if you manufacture the products and the only labour used is yours, you should still track runs and consider your full salary, regardless of whether you're paid or not. This ensures you are creating accurate margin information on which to build your business. Here is an example of how you might track your landed costs:

Landed cost tracker

Batch	Cost	Freight	Qty	Landed
001	$500	$100	500	$1.200
002	$750	$110	750	$1.146
003	$350	$100	300	$1.500

Once you have your landed costs, you want to take the goods cost for each production run, add your hours spent and times it by your hourly rate to get your total cost. Once you have the total cost of the run, you can simply divide the full cost by the final yield to get your cost of goods. Here is a basic example:

Production tracking example

Batch	Goods	Labour	Expected Yield	Actual Yield	Unit Cost
001	$50	$100	1,000	990	$0.152
002	$100	$190	2,000	2,005	$0.145
003	$25	$90	500	505	$0.228

As you can see, the unit cost varies dramatically, depending on the labour and yield, even if the goods cost remains consistent to the expected yield. By tracking the costs for every batch, we can better understand what our margin is over time.

CALCULATING YOUR MARGIN

The tools above will get you your cost of goods, and from here you can calculate your margins. If you have already set your pricing, the formula is very straightforward. You should calculate your margin using the net sell price, exclusive of any taxes. It is critical you know your operational margin for context in future chapters.

$$Margin = \frac{NetPrice - Cost}{NetPrice}$$

If you haven't yet set your pricing, you have the opportunity to build in the margin you need. You can do this by either work-ing towards a target sell price or working towards a target cost price. I have built some online calculators to help with this, which you can access at this link: https://jasonstockton.com.au/calculator/margin/

Another layer of complexity comes in when you have a retail price, wholesale price and, potentially, distributor price. Each of these will have a different margin. Each tier can also drive a different retail price, based on the margin required for each channel as they compound. To help with this, I have built these scenarios into the online calculators to help you build your pricing.

Once you've built and established your margin, you need to remain flexible with it. Costs will vary and customer expectations will evolve. In the next chapter, we'll figure out what margin your business actually needs.

CHAPTER REVISION

- What is the difference between accounting margin and operational margin?
- What is your preferred method to calculate your landed cost?
- What is your average cost of goods?
- What is your margin for each sales channel?
- How will you track this accurately on an ongoing basis?

CHAPTER 3

MARGIN MEETS VOLUME: CAN THIS BE A GOOD BUSINESS?

This is a question we should be asking ourselves more often than we do. The reality of business is that the best product does not equal a good business. In the same way, a high margin product also does not equal a good business. So how do we find out if we have a good, profitable business?

There are two essential factors – our margin and volume. If you have an expensive product, you will commonly have a lower volume. This means that the margin has to be higher to cover the operational expenses. Conversely, if you have a high-volume product, you can get away with a much lower margin because the volume covers the lack of margin.

FINDING YOUR BREAK-EVEN VOLUME

Depending on the product you sell, there will be a volume + margin sweet spot you need to find. This will give you, first, your break-even point, then, at higher volumes, your profitability. To work this out, we need to take our unit margin and average sell price, then use these numbers to establish what volume we have to achieve to break even.

The formula to work out how many units must be sold to break even is relatively straightforward. Take your total OPEX (this excludes the cost of goods) and divide it by your average margin dollars (average sell price minus the cost of goods).

$$BreakEven = \frac{Operating Expenses}{Sell Price - Cost Of Goods}$$

You can also use our online calculator to work out your profitability point, as well as what profit you would make for any given volume:
https://jasonstockton.com.au/calculator/profitability/

I find that using how many units you need to sell is a more useful metric than revenue to understand whether the business is viable. You can also get a more in-depth understanding of whether the market you're targeting is too small, and whether the sales channels you're looking at make sense. Revenue numbers are intangible and aspirational; we can easily be deluded by following them. Unit metrics don't allow that same delusion because they are very real and tangible.

Let's look at a few different scenarios. Firstly, if you need to sell 33,000 units of a product to break even, but can only produce 20,000 a year, that is a bad business that will only lead to significant losses.

Capacity lower than profitability

Cost of Goods	$5
Sell Price	$20
Margin Dollars	$15
Operating Expenses	$500,000
Required Units	**33,000**
Unit Capacity	**20,000**
Net Profit	**-$200,000**

You can also try to understand the demand for your product to see if you can make money from the business. For example, if you need to sell 30,000 units, but you think realistically there is only demand for 10,000 units, you're basically throwing away money.

Demand lower than profitability

Cost of Goods	$3
Sell Price	$10
Margin Dollars	$7
Operating Expenses	$210,000
Required Units	**30,000**
Unit Demand	**10,000**
Net Profit	**-$140,000**

You could, however, be onto a winner when the demand is high, it's easy to produce and expenses are manageable. If you only need to sell 20,000 units and actually sell 50,000 units, then you will have to invest in some new pants with deep pockets that can fit all your extra cash.

Sales higher than required

Cost of Goods	$10
Sell Price	$25
Margin Dollars	$15
Operating Expenses	$300,000
Required Units	**20,000**
Unit Sales	**50,000**
Net Profit	**$450,000**

It is easy to lose money in business – 60% of businesses fail in the first 5 years, and even of those that survive, almost half never make a profit. Of course, when you're starting out you need to invest and the opportunity could be huge. However, if you can eliminate some risk by doing this profitability check upfront, you will save yourself a lot of pain in the long run. It also pays to get the margins and OPEX as accurate as you can so that these formulas give you a true indication of your business.

FINDING YOUR RIGHT MARGIN

With this data in hand, we want to work out what margin and volume is achievable and realistic. As mentioned in the previous chapter, the highest margin is not always the best business strategy.

Let's take a chocolate bar, for example. If the average competing chocolate bar costs $5 and yours is $10, the reality is, your product is going to move at a far lower volume. Even if it tastes twice as good, the majority of consumers cannot justify a purchase twice the price.

If the product costs us $3 to make, and we sell it whole-sale at $6, we have a 50% margin when sold at wholesale. If we're moving 10,000 bars, we're making $30,000 – however, if our OPEX is $50,000, we're making a $20,000 loss.

Theoretical sales Example 1

Cost of Goods	$3
Wholesale Price	$6
Retail Price	$10
Unit Sales	10,000
Gross Profit	**$30,000**
OPEX	**$50,000**
Profit	**-$20,000**

The commonly considered solution to this problem is to spend more on marketing. The issue with that is that it's high risk and unlikely to solve the issue because we're adding more expenses, compounding our losses. An alternative strategy would be sacrificing some margin so we can move some vol-ume. It sounds counterintuitive, but the math makes sense.

If we drop our margin to just 30%, it has a compounding effect on our retail price. The wholesale price comes down to $4.29, with the retailers maintaining 40% margin, and the sell price is now $7.15. From a consumer perspective, the product is still premium, but it is a justifiable price difference. Now, in-stead of buying one sporadically, they will buy multiple more frequently. With a low estimate of sales going 5x without any additional investment, your income is now $64,500. With our OPEX unchanged, we now make $14,500 in profit.

Theoretical sales Example 2

Cost of Goods	$3
Wholesale Price	$4.29
Retail Price	$7.15
Unit Sales	50,000
Gross Profit	**$64,500**
OPEX	**$50,000**
Profit	**$14,500**

As volumes climb, the economics shift in your favour. You unlock bulk discounts, automation becomes viable and shipping rates drop. You traded margin for volume initially, and now volume gives you back the margin.

Now, of course, there are scenarios in which a great brand can sell at a high margin and still achieve good volume. So, the pricing strategy you choose will heavily depend on the achievable volumes and price points that make sense for you.

CHAPTER REVISION

- Based on your margins and OPEX, what volume do you need to break even?
- How profitable can the business be, and does the business make sense to pursue?
- Is the volume achievable at the product's price point and sales channel mix?
- If you adjust your margin, can you achieve more sales or more profit?

CHAPTER 4

THE THREE SCENARIOS THAT SAVE BUSINESSES: FORECAST YOUR WAY TO UNDERSTANDING

We've established our margins, break-even volumes and profitability targets. The next step is building the forecasts that can guide us on how to reach those targets.

In the past, I found forecasting pointless. It took ages to build a forecast, and it was just a guess anyway. For a long time, I didn't do it, and that was a mistake. A mentor told me I *had* to forecast and once I did it, everything changed. It's not so much about predicting the future, it's more about using it as a guide to understand what is achievable for your business and know where you are in relation to it.

I've found the most useful way to forecast is to build them for three scenarios.

- Your best-case scenario: what happens if the business beats all of your expectations.
- Your realistic scenario: what you're realistically expecting to happen.

- Your worst-case scenario: what happens if the sh!t hits the fan.

The reason for doing all three is that it makes you consider how you would handle each scenario.

- In your best-case scenario, how will you produce and distribute the amount of product you need?
- Is your realistic scenario profitable? Do the volumes make sense based on available resources?
- In the worst-case scenario, how will you stay afloat? How do you get things back on track?

When you have answers and plans for each scenario, you will be able to react faster with less stress because you were prepared for the situation.

BUILDING THE REVENUE FORECAST

To build your forecast, you will first need to start with a template (or build your own). I have a free template that you can download at this link: https://jasonstockton.com.au/template/forecast/

If you prefer to create your own, you can follow these steps. The first sheet of the template should cover at least a year's worth of forecasted sales. You can either list this as daily or weekly sales, depending on your preference for tracking. Monthly is too short as you will be too slow to react to where you sit against the forecast. We'll work with weeks for our examples.

The top line of the forecast should be your actual net sales, which you will fill out based on the actual weeks' performance.

The next row is reserved for your forecasted sales revenue (usually in net sales, exclusive of tax). The unit volume can be calculated from your sales based on the actual week's or day's performance, or you can forecast the sales revenue based on the unit volume expected.

The next rows should cover your cost of goods. The easiest way to calculate this is by making it a percentage of sales revenue, or the number of units times the average cost of goods. If you have multiple sales channels, you need to work out an expected average between all sales channels. The revenue less your cost of goods establishes your gross profit.

The next rows will be your expected OPEX. This includes rent, salaries (excluding those we've considered in our cost of goods), freight, utilities, insurance, marketing, etc.

There are two types of expenses to consider: variable and fixed. Variable expenses will be expenses that change, depending on the volume. These could be freight, marketing and other expenses linked to revenue volumes. You can set variable expenses up as a percentage of your overall net sales so they adjust relative to the revenue. Fixed expenses will be those that are set and not dependent on volume. These could be rent, utilities, insurance and other expenses that are static, regardless of volumes. It is worthwhile calculating your yearly cost for these and dividing it equally across each of the weeks. This avoids constant fluctuations in your net profit in the forecasts.

You want to forecast all of your expenses as best you can, relative to the scenario you're forecasting for. Your gross profit less any expenses will give you your net profit. You may have weeks forecasted to make a loss, and others that are profitable. Overall, for the full year you would like to be profitable – otherwise, what is the point?

Financial forecast example

FY	Week 1	Week 2	Week 3	Week 4
Actual Sales	$16,927	$13,874		
Forecasted Sales	$15,000	$14,500	$16,000	$17,500
Units Sold	1,627	1,387	1,600	1,750
Cost of Goods	$5,078	$4,162	$4,800	$5,250
Gross Profit	**$11,849**	**$9,712**	**$11,200**	**$12,250**
Expenses:				
Marketing	$2,000	$2,000	$2,500	$2,500
Rent	$1,000	$1,000	$1,000	$1,000
Salaries	$5,000	$5,000	$5,000	$5,000
Software	$400	$400	$400	$400
Utilities	$400	$400	$400	$400
Insurance	$300	$300	$300	$300
Freight	$338	$277	$320	$350
Other	$150	$150	$150	$150
Total Expenses	**$9,588**	**$9,527**	**$9,570**	**$9,600**
Net Profit	**$2,261**	**$185**	**$1,630**	**$2,900**

Try not to under forecast. Although it feels good to beat your forecast, low forecasts also prevent you from trying harder and your actual result will end up lower than you probably could have achieved if you aimed higher. Make sure your realistic forecast is hard but achievable. You'll be surprised what you can achieve when you push yourself.

With the forecast completed, you should sanity check that your estimated volumes and margins from the previous chapters still make sense. You may find that your OPEX has changed, therefore overall volumes and profitability points have moved. This may mean that you need a higher margin or volume to break even.

FORECASTING CAPACITY

You're not done yet though. We now need to forecast our capacity based on each forecast. The unit sales is important because it gives you an idea of how much stock you need at any given point. If you don't have enough stock, you won't be able to hit your sales targets. If you are manufacturing the product yourself, you will be able to forecast what to produce and when. If you have a third-party manufacturer, you can provide them with the forecasts to help with their planning.

On the second sheet of the spreadsheet, we will take the unit volumes for each week and establish our requirements for stock. Using this number, we can layer in our actual capacity to see if we can meet the demand. It is critical to check this against our best-case scenario as well as our realistic scenario, to ensure we can actually achieve both.

In the first row, we will add our capacity for each week. The capacity may be static or it may flex, based on staff availability and supply. The next row will pull in the unit sales from the previous sheet. Below this, we will record how many units we plan to produce or did produce for the week. The final row is our running stock tally that will take the previous week's stock level, subtract the units sold and add the units produced. This will help us plan for dealing with periods during which sales outperform capacity by ensuring we have enough coverage for those periods.

Capacity forecast example

FY	Week 1	Week 2	Week 3	Week 4
Capacity	2,000	2,000	2,000	2,000
Units Sold	1,627	1,387	1,600	1,750
Units Produced	1,600	1,600	1,600	1,600
Running Stock	**2,000**	**2,213**	**2,213**	**2,063**

$$RunningStock = PreviousRunningStock - UnitsSold + UnitsProduced$$

If you have perishable stock, then you need to ensure your running stock factors in the shelf life of the product you have. The downloadable template mentioned at the start of this chapter allows you to enter a shelf life in weeks and handles the complex formula for you. If you have a large product range, you will want to do some extra ranging work to understand the product mix that makes up this unit volume. Then, you can plan to have the right products behind these units. You can use your weeks on hand report to assist with this. We will touch on that more in later chapters.

FOLLOWING YOUR FORECAST

It is one thing to build the forecast, but the most important thing is to know where you stack up against it. You should make a habit of tracking your sales against the forecast on either a daily or weekly basis. Do not consider any longer periods than that because it will be too late to react. The frequency and consistency is crucial because it will enable you to know where you are at any given point. In some weeks you may be hitting your realistic target and in others you may be in your best-case or worst-case scenarios. You need to ensure you action the requirements for where you are.

Tip: To help you stay on track, it is great to schedule weekly meetings with key team members to share the performance against the forecast. This will help you follow and discuss the results regularly, and it will bring your team along the journey with you.

Keep in mind that the forecast is only a guide. Your expenses will vary, your unit volumes won't be perfect and your margins may change. You will still need to read your P&L regularly to see where you've actually landed each month. Think of the forecast more as a map to help keep you on track towards your destination. We'll be referring back to the forecast a lot as we look to optimise the sh!t in the middle.

CHAPTER REVISION

- What is your best-case, realistic and worst-case scenario forecast for the next year?
- Is there enough capacity, or can you plan to scale your capacity to meet all scenarios, including the best-case?
- How frequently will you update the forecast with actual sales?
- Do you have a plan for how you will survive during a worst-case scenario?

CHAPTER 5

THE 450-MINUTE WORKDAY: OPTIMISING YOUR CAPACITY

If you manufacture products yourself, your capacity for how much you can manufacture is critical to your success. Although getting the sales can be difficult, if you succeed you will quickly reach limitations with your capacity.

In this chapter, I will provide some tips on how to manage and optimise your capacity to get the maximum output.

HUMAN CAPACITY

In many countries, salaries are the highest cost in the business. Regardless of this, many business owners have a habit of hiring extra staff to increase capacity, instead of optimising the business processes. This is expensive and is effectively burning cash and throwing away any potential profits.

Instead, you should look to optimise the output of every team member and minimise the number of staff needed in the business. A great way to look at it is to understand how many working minutes there are in a day. A 7.5-hour workday equals 450 usable minutes of labour. If your processes waste just 30 minutes of that time a day, it equates to 7,800 minutes a year, or over 17 days' worth of labour down the drain! This is the silent killer for most businesses, because often there is a lot more than 30 minutes a day being wasted.

Think about your worst employee. We all know who the biggest problem is in our business at any given time. What you need to establish is the "why". Are they a bad culture fit, a toxic human, slow or disinterested? Bad culture fit and toxicity are clear signs to fire, if you can, but for all other scenarios you need to consider some other options.

As a business owner and manager, you're typically used to things being done at a certain pace. Typically, the pace that you set is based on what you can personally achieve doing that given task. The harsh reality is, though, that it is rare to find employees who will be self-motivated and work consistently at the pace you want. This is an expectation that we as owners and managers need to accept, because they are unlikely to have the same level of passion and dedication as us, whether they love the job or not.

Once you've accepted that, you have to ensure that you are not the problem. The way you do something as an owner or manager is not necessarily the most efficient way for a team member to do it. Often, your processes don't factor in one critical piece of information: Humans can only do 3 to 4 hours of critical thinking a day.

Typically, business owners and managers can break this rule because we're already wired to work in this way so it requires less critical thinking and more general thinking. But for everyone else the processes typically require a lot of critical thinking, so an employee is drained every day, to the point where they burn out, and the job becomes less fun, and more of a chore. To avoid this, you need to aim to remove as much critical thinking from all the processes within the business as possible.

Let me give you a common example. Most businesses start with paper-based pick and pack processes. Picking an order requires a team member to read the item and the quantity required, and then grab the right one that corresponds with the text. They need to double-check they picked the correct amount, then send it to the correct address with the right shipping label. While the process is easy to understand, we have all experienced staff picking the wrong items or mixing up the shipping labels. We tell them off, or encourage them to do better, but nothing ever changes. The worst part is, it ALWAYS happens when we're at our busiest. That sale that drove a lot of revenue is now going to cost us a bunch more dollars, fixing up all the messed-up orders and upset customers.

But if you flip the script and look at the process, it requires a lot of critical thinking. When things get busy, the pressure increases. They want to ship more orders for you, but the reality is that there is too much reliance on the human. Now sure, you can add a second check during packing and separate the processes. I tried that, and it helped, but errors continued to occur. Not only that, but it was terribly inefficient. You're unable to maximise the number of hours in the day because mistakes inevitably creep in. Take a look at this example.

Manual process

Time Per Order	10 minutes
Usable Hours	4 hours
Maximum Output	24 orders

All that thinking adds time. Given that critical thinking is used up within 4 hours, if it takes 10 minutes to pick an order, we can only complete 24 orders per day before mistakes creep in. *That's on a good day!*

Fortunately, there is a solution: introduce personal digital assistant (PDA) scanners for the pick and pack. Now the user is guided through the warehouse efficiently and pictures enable the user to quickly match the item. When the user scans the item, it will automatically confirm if it is the right item and quantity (or the wrong one). Now it's faster, and because the scanners and barcodes are doing the critical thinking, we are not burning out the staff member and we are preventing mistakes.

Digitally assisted process

Time Per Order	7 minutes
Usable Hours	7.5 hours
Maximum Output	64 orders

Now with this new process, we have gone from 24 orders a day to 64 orders. When we went from paper to digital in my chocolate business, we went from around a 1–2% error rate to virtually no errors. The team member would have to royally mess up to make a mistake.

If you have a large range of products, you can also consider alternative picking strategies to optimise even further. Here are some common methods to look at.

Single pick

This is usually where you start, picking one order at a time. This is useful for low order volumes, small product ranges or large orders.

Cluster picking

This is when you have a trolley with multiple "tubs" on it, each tub associated with an order, and you walk through the warehouse in sequence and pick the specific items for each tub. The tubs arrive at the pack station already separated, ready for packing. This is useful for high-volume and larger product ranges.

Batch picking

This is when you pick all the stock you need for multiple orders at once. These would then be sorted into their specific order during packing. This is useful for smaller product ranges or easily distinguished items. Often this is the least efficient method due to double handling and a large reliance on critical thinking.

Zone picking

This is when you pick in "zones" for example, all the products would be picked from Zone A and B by different pickers, then usually sent to a pack station via conveyor to be combined and shipped. This is useful for giant warehouses with long walking distances.

Not all picking methods will be supported by all PDA scanner software options. Be sure to do your research to ensure you find the right software for you and your industry. I'll have some tips on how to find the right software for you later in the book.

Now, let's say we adopted cluster picking in the scenario above and we were able to drop our picking time per order down to just 5 minutes.

Digitally assisted process with cluster picking

Time Per Order	5 minutes
Usable Hours	7.5 hours
Maximum Output	90 orders

Now we can get 90 orders out a day per person. We've halved our pick and pack time, increased our usable time and reduced errors and we can now deliver over 3.7 times the orders.

This is just one process example. In your business you will likely have loads of other processes, from order input to stock receiving. If you apply this same thinking to EVERY process in your business and eliminate critical thinking, you will dramatically increase output without increasing your headcount.

Here is a list of processes you can look at optimising, in the same way we have reviewed the pick and pack process. You may not have all of these functions in your business, but find the relevant ones and optimise them:

- Purchasing
- Production runs
- Pick and pack
- Reconciling purchase orders
- Sales order data entry
- Customer support
- Sales
- Production scheduling
- Reporting
- Quality and safety controls
- Stocktaking
- Price management
- Order allocation

-   Last mile delivery
-   Stock transfers
-   Recipe costings
-   Batch tracking
-   Accounting
-   Expense management
-   Supplier management
-   Product management
-   Pick-up orders
-   Invoicing
-   Write-offs and wastage

PHYSICAL SPACE

Another capacity constraint comes in the form of physical space. You only have so much space and as you grow you will eventually outgrow the space and need a larger facility. The challenge here is that every time you need to upgrade or move, it costs time and money – a lot of time and money. With this in mind, you also have to optimise your space.

Use existing shelving

The first way to maximise space is to use shelving effectively. Try to minimise the gaps between the shelves to remove as much empty space as possible. If you're able to get an extra shelf within a bay, it makes a massive difference to the overall space.

Use height

Don't forget to look up. Most warehouses are tall, and often you only use shelving within reach. However, investing in an appropriate ladder, forklift or scissor lift to reach higher shelving is far cheaper than moving. To do this effectively, you would keep high-volume items within arm's reach to maintain efficiency for your teams. Additional stock that is not regularly required can go up higher and only get pulled down when needed.

You can also look at building in a mezzanine. It doesn't come cheap, but it can allow you to almost double your storage space while keeping items within arm's reach. During my time at PUMA, we moved warehouses three times. Each warehouse had a different set-up, based on the warehouse manager's preference. The last warehouse ended up as a hybrid of the two approaches mentioned above. A section of large bulk storage went high up to the ceiling, and another multi-level section was used for picking stock without the need for ladders or forklifts. As stock was depleted from the multi-level section, bulk storage was brought down to refill the picking bay. Ultimately, the approach you take will depend on your product, sales channels and pick preferences.

Temporary overflow storage

If you're bursting at the seams at peak times, consider using temporary container storage in your car park or a nearby storage facility. These can give you the extra space to deal with seasonal demand, without paying for a whole new warehouse which is only full part of the time. Get as creative as you can to delay moving as long as you can.

Minimise stock on hand

Another option is to keep stock levels to a minimum by using the just-in-time philosophy. Just-in-time refers to having the stock ready "just-in-time" for production or dispatch so the stock is not held for very long. This is great when it works because it frees up both space and cash. It does, however, run the risk of running out of stock when you most need it.

Reduce walking distances

You need to also consider distance. The best warehouses and production facilities in the world have a flow to them. Stock will be received directly to where it is needed, so production or picking teams can effectively grab what they need without walking great distances. Then your distance from production to picking and eventually dispatch needs to be carefully considered. If you can have stock received next to the production, then finished goods stored between production and picking teams, this creates a smooth flow for your stock from start to finish. If each team member wastes time walking unnecessary distances, this has a large, compounding cost on your business.

If you run a production facility, then use this same philosophy of minimal movement within your production space. You want to ensure you are minimising the movement and distance for every task. An improvement of just a few minutes a day could ultimately save you thousands of dollars over the course of a year. We'll discuss some more ways to optimise your production output later on.

CHAPTER REVISION

- What are all the functions and processes in your business?
- Are you using all available 450 minutes per employee effectively?
- How can each of these processes be optimised to make them more efficient and reduce critical thinking?
- How can your space be optimised to maximise storage capacity?
- How can you better lay out the space to minimise the movement and time spent within the facility?
- Are there ways to automate any manual manufacturing processes?
- Does contract manufacturing make sense for your product?

CHAPTER 6

STOCK IS CASH YOU CAN'T SPEND: MINIMISING YOUR STOCK ON HAND

Your stock is both an asset and a risk to your business. You will often have too much of some products and not enough of others. This is a constant juggling act you need to watch closely, because stock is money tied up that you can't spend until you sell it.

It is important to know your stock value as both a cost and a retail value at all times. The cost value lets you know how much cash is physically tied up in stock, while the retail value gives you potential revenue that can be made from the stock on hand. Many businesses don't track this well or at all, and they're playing a dangerous game. Too much stock and your cash flow is killed, not enough stock and revenue will suffer. Using this data in tandem with your forecast is the best way to ensure you have the right amount of stock at the right time.

UNDERSTANDING STOCK TURNS

Your stock turn is a critical number. It is effectively the measure of how frequently your entire stock turns over each year. The number depends on the product you sell and the industry you're in. For example, if you have a perishable product that only lasts a month, the minimum stock turn you would want is 12. However, you would likely target something much higher than that to ensure you're always providing the freshest stock to customers. Below is a guide you can use for various industries.

Target stock turns

Industry	Stock Turn
Grocery/Perishables	12–20+
Fast Fashion	4–6+
Consumer Electronics	6–10
General Retail/Hardware	3–5
Luxury Goods/High End	1–3
Manufacturing	5–10

So, how do you calculate your stock turn? Simply divide the last 12 months' COGS by the current cost value of your inventory. For example, if your COGS for the last 12 months was $1,000,000, and you currently hold $250,000 worth of stock, then your stock turn would be 4.

$$StockTurn = \frac{CostOfGoodsSold}{InventoryCostValue}$$

If your stock turn is within the acceptable range (or higher), then your business will be generally healthy. As long as you're not constantly out of stock, a high stock turn is a great outcome. Conversely, if your stock turn is lower than what it should be for your industry, then it means you're holding too much stock.

Earlier I mentioned the just-in-time philosophy – if you use this methodology, you can use the stock turn to measure how "just-in-time" you actually are.

OPTIMISING YOUR STOCK LEVELS

There are several ways to optimise your stock levels. In the age of AI, modern software or ERP software can do a lot of the heavy lifting when trying to forecast future sales to help establish how much stock you need. Whether this is useful or not really depends on the industry you're in. Some industries are highly predictable and based on seasonality. Others are volatile and challenging to predict.

The best way to work out your stock position by product is to use a "weeks on hand" report (you can also do a "days on hand" or "months on hand" report, depending on the product and industry). Modern operational ERP software, like Supply'd, will have these reports built in, but if you don't have software like this, it is not overly difficult to build.

To build a weeks on hand report, you need to calculate your rate of sale (ROS) for each product. A simple way to do this is to take the last 7 days of units sold and use that as your current ROS. If you want to average it out based on a longer period, you could, for example, take the last 70 days of units sold and divide it by 70 to get your daily ROS, then times it by 7 for the weeks. Some more advanced methods include using AI forecasts or a moving average to forecast the future ROS.

If you would like to do a days on hand or months on hand report, you will need to adjust the period from 7 days to one day or 30/31 days. Once you have your ROS, you want to take your current stock on hand and divide it by the ROS.

$$WeeksOnHand = \frac{CurrentStockOnHand}{RateOfSale}$$

For example, if you have 100 units in stock, and your current ROS is 15, you will have 6.66 weeks' worth of stock. This report is commonly used by businesses around the world to work out what products they have too much or too little of. If your weeks on hand for a given product is high, you have too much stock, and it is tying up capital. If this is the case, consider clearing this stock somehow. Conversely, if the weeks on hand is low, you need to get more stock in urgently to avoid losing sales.

Tip: Consider including additional details in this report, like the shelf life for perishable products or lead time, so you can make sure you're always in stock of bestsellers and not over stocked with slow sellers.

Keeping on top of stock through the weeks on hand report will maximise your stock turn number and hopefully free up some cash flow and maximise sales to ensure you have a healthy business.

DEALING WITH RETURNS

In some industries in parts of the world, returns can reach as high as 30% for online businesses, particularly in fashion. Some brands I have worked with have around a 10% return rate and offer generous 60-day free returns. While this is great for the consumer, it is dangerous for the business. You're footing the bill for the stock to come back, you're paying to check the stock and refund the customer, and the last oddment (an odd size that isn't sold yet) is now back in your warehouse taking up space. So now you've paid for the goods, shipping out and the shipping back to the warehouse and the cost to process it, all basically for free. It is an absolute nightmare.

If you're going to trade online, it is a reality, and you need to tread carefully. Large businesses can afford to be generous with their terms, as they have the margin and profitability there to cover the loss. If you're a small business, you don't have that luxury, so how do you meet customer expectations without sending yourself out of business?

REVIEW YOUR MARGINS

If you are in an industry with high returns, you need to make sure you have the margin to cover it. Fashion is a promotionally-led industry, which means you're often selling discounted (eating your margin) and then offering things like free shipping and free returns to get the sale through. Most of the global brands work with very generous margins of 70 to 90%, so when an item is 50% off, they still make considerable margins on their products.

Typical footwear pricing

	Value	Margin
Cost of Goods	$35	-
Retail Price	$200	83%
Sale Price	$100	65%

They can do this because they have built the brand and reputation and have set the value of the product over a long period of time. Once the product goes on sale, they know they will still make good money and be able to cover the cost of any returns. So how can you make sure you're covering these costs? Let's use the example above, where they have a 65% margin and use $100,000 of sales with a 10% return rate.

Return calculation with high margin

	Value	Margin
Revenue	$100,000	-
Margin	$65,000	65%
Outbound Shipping Costs	$15,000	15%
Gross Profit	**$50,000**	**50%**
Returns	$10,000	10%
Return Shipping Costs	$1,500	15%
Processing Costs	$500	5%
Gross Profit	**$38,000**	**38%**

You can see there is still a healthy gross profit at this level. Even after the returns and shipping costs have been covered, there is a 38% margin to work with. The challenge comes in when you have a low margin product or a higher return rate. Let's use an example with a 40% margin and 20% return rate.

Return calculation with low margin

	Value	Margin
Revenue	$100,000	-
Margin	$40,000	40%
Outbound Shipping Costs	$15,000	15%
Gross Profit	**$25,000**	**25%**
Returns	$20,000	20%
Return Shipping Costs	$3,000	15%
Processing Costs	$1,000	5%
Gross Profit	**$1,000**	**1%**

Now you're left just 1% of margin to cover your OPEX, and you're going to be burning cash faster than Elon Musk trying to fix Twitter (now X). It's worthwhile doing this analysis early and working out if your business is able to offer free returns, or if you even need an online store at all.

Although online is a popular place to shop, it does not always make fiscal sense. It is expensive to operate, and you will need to spend a fortune on marketing, and here's what most people won't tell you – you usually won't make money selling online unless you can achieve high volumes. This then goes back to the work we did on margins and profitability points to make sure online is the right channel for you. And before you say, "Fine, I'll open a retail store", you need to do the math here as well. Although the return volumes are much lower, your fixed costs are much higher to cover rent and staffing, so again, you require the volume to justify it. Wholesale, albeit with its lower margin, is the lowest risk channel in which to start getting volume. It does, however, depend on the product, industry, and volumes that you're able to achieve, so do your homework based on the tool kit I've given you.

HAVE A CLEAR PLAN FOR ODD STOCK

Oddments and returned stock tied up in a warehouse become a real problem fast. You need to have a plan to clear them out regularly so they don't get out of control. Consider some of these ideas to keep this stock moving:

- Sell the items for cheap online with a "no returns" policy.
- Sell at cost through clearance wholesalers (but note that many don't accept oddments, and they require a good size profile and depth to accept them).
- Give them away to a charity.
- Recycle or dispose of them thoughtfully.

Dead stock will cost you in the long run; take the hit so it stops occupying unnecessary space in your warehouse.

CHAPTER REVISION

- What is your current stock on hand value at cost and at retail?
- Does this stock level make sense, based on your forecast?
- What is your current stock turn?
- What is the weeks on hand of your product range, and is there any high-risk stock that needs to be dealt with?
- Are returns an issue for your industry? How much margin will they eat up?
- Do you have a plan to clear out odd sizes and slow sellers?

CHAPTER 7

VOLUME BUYS YOU LEVERAGE: OPTIMISING YOUR SUPPLY CHAIN

Your supply chain is effectively a fancy word for your suppliers and inbound freight. It's all about getting the stock into your hands. Your supply chain is a critical piece to get right because it can have a massive impact on your costs, capacity and quality. The wrong partner can ultimately break your business.

CHOOSING THE RIGHT SUPPLIER

Finding the appropriate supplier to work with is an ongoing project until you find what you need. While shopping for a good price is important, you need to balance that with the right quality product to meet your requirements, but also the reliability of the supply and delivery. There is no point having the best price if the product you require is constantly out of stock.

It pays to shop around and get at least three quotes, more if you can. Your initial decision will be based on gut feel of what works for you. After you have worked with the supplier for a period of time you will have a more in-depth understanding of the reliability of supply. Don't burn bridges with the other suppliers, because you will need a back-up in case one supplier is out of stock. It is common for larger businesses to have three to five suppliers for a given product to ensure a steady flow of stock. If your primary supplier is out of stock, try your secondary suppliers to ensure your business is not disrupted.

Depending on the industry, you may start out buying from importers and distributors. These are often pricier than buying direct from a manufacturer, but until you have sufficient volume, you won't be able to buy direct. ERP and procurement software can monitor how much you're purchasing and using each year so you can use this information to have conversations with direct manufacturers. You can sometimes save up to 50%, depending on the mark up of your distributor. I've heard of businesses saving as much as $100,000 a year on just one ingredient!

CASH IS KING

Getting payment terms with your suppliers is one of the best ways to help with cash flow in a business. If you can buy stock now and not have to pay for it until after you've sold it, then your cash flow will be golden.

When you're first starting a business, you have no credit history, therefore no room to negotiate things like payment terms. This quickly becomes a chicken and egg scenario, in which you can't get terms because you've never had terms. To get your first terms with a supplier, you should build a good relationship with them, paying on delivery initially if you have to. Once you have the relationship, often you can get 7-day terms to start with. This allows you 7 days to pay the invoice from the invoice date. From here, you can work with the supplier to extend that over time as the relationship evolves and volumes increase. Most businesses max out at around 30 to 60 days payment terms. You may also come across end of month (EOM) terms. For example, 14 days EOM means you have 14 days from the last day of the month in which the invoice was issued to pay. To take full advantage of EOM terms, aim to buy early in the month. This gives you the longest possible window to pay.

Another option that helps with cash flow is to consider a credit card. Credit cards can offer up to 55 days to pay, so if you have terms and a credit card, you can extend the amount of time you have to pay for stock even further. This does come at a price, though. Most suppliers will on-charge their credit card surcharge to you, meaning your stock will be costing you more, and you need to factor this into your cost of goods. The other "gotcha" is that if you fail to pay on time, you will get stung with costly interest fees.

NEGOTIATING AND VOLUME BUYING

The payment term available is really up to the supplier and your negotiating skills. Payment terms are a risk to the supplier, so you need something to give in return – generally speaking, that would be volume. The more you buy regularly, the more you can negotiate terms.

Remember, this is a two-way street – you need to offer something in terms of volume and regularity to justify the request to the supplier. This is where your forecasting is beneficial. Planning ahead lets you better understand the volumes that you require and you can share these with your suppliers to get the best rate. It can be beneficial here to use your best-case scenario for negotiation, as long as it is not completely out of reach. The benefit of using these numbers means the supplier is prepared for your best-case scenario, and you will get the best price. Most suppliers will be lenient on the achieved volumes, provided it is a good long-term relationship and you are paying on time. If you can order higher volumes in one order (by pallet or container), you will also be able to get either free or lower shipping rates. Be careful not to over-stock, though, as this ties up your cash.

MANAGING FREIGHT

If you buy locally, freight is manageable. It can easily be worked into your landed cost of goods. If you import goods from overseas, this is much harder. Some overseas products might seem cheap, but when you've factored in freight, costs jump. It might still be cheaper than buying locally, but then the stock lands on shore and you get slammed with extra duties, taxes and delivery charges. All of a sudden, those freight costs have blown out and your margin has dwindled.

When your overseas supplier provides a quote on freight, they will provide the International Commercial Terms (Incoterms) for which they are being fulfilled. Understanding these terms and what they mean is crucial. These terms define who is responsible for what part of the delivery.

Incoterm glossary

Incoterm	What it actually means
Ex Works (EXW)	You pick it up from their factory floor.
Free on Board (FOB)	Supplier handles everything until it sits on the ship.
Cost, Insurance, Freight (CIF)	The supplier pays to get it to your local port, but YOU take the risk once it's on the boat.
Delivered At Place (DAP)	Supplier pays to deliver to your door, you pay any import taxes.
Delivered Duty Paid (DDP)	Supplier handles absolutely everything, including taxes.

If you're just starting out and want to avoid using freight forwarders, DDP is often your best option. It will cost you more upfront, but it will save you a lot of hassle that comes with international freight. If you would rather not pay the premium, then it is worth working with a freight forwarder to make the process easier. International freight is extremely complicated and unless you have experience in this industry, leave it to the experts so you can get back to optimising the sh!t in the middle.

CHAPTER REVISION

- Who is the best supplier for your product/each component?
- Do you have any back-up suppliers in case of supply issues?
- What are the best payment terms you can achieve with your suppliers?
- Does a credit card make sense for your business, to help with cash flow?
- Does volume buying help you get a better price and/or payment terms with your suppliers?
- If you're importing from overseas, what Incoterm option is being offered by the supplier?
- What is the total freight likely to add to the cost of goods of this item?

CHAPTER 8

WHEN TO FIRE CUSTOMERS: OPTIMISING YOUR CUSTOMERS

Not all business customers are created equal. Some will ask for unreasonable terms, others will need low rates for crazy volumes. It is rare you find a customer who is willing to pay whatever you ask and give you volume at the same time. This is normal, and it is much the same as when you negotiate for better deals with your suppliers. It is part of being a good operator.

There is a danger that many small businesses fall into, where they are simply unwilling to negotiate. Usually, this comes from a lack of understanding of their numbers (thinking any discount will bankrupt them), or assuming the customer won't pay if they give terms. The reality is that in business we are taking risks all the time – you took a risk when you started the business and put your money into it. You need to take these risks to further the business. Now, of course, you shouldn't blindly agree to what a customer is asking, but you should be willing to negotiate. Much like your negotiations with your suppliers, if your customers want generous terms or low prices, they need to deliver on the volume. Because you have done the work in the early chapters of this book, you understand what your margins are and where your profitability point is. Now you can make an educated call on whether the deal makes sense for you or not.

FINDING YOUR COST TO SERVE

Cost to serve is understanding the real cost to service a customer. Unfortunately, not all customers are profitable customers. You'll have some customers who often buy a large amount and who need little customer support. Then you may have others who buy very little, infrequently, and yet need the most customer support. You may also come across bad payers who don't pay on time – they really kill your cash flow.

Every transaction has a cost beyond the cost of goods. That can be time to input the order, time spent on the phone (especially if it's you) and time fulfilling the order. All of this eats into the margin for the customer. If you have a customer like this, then it is worthwhile doing a cost to serve analysis. If you use software like an ERP you can usually access your exact margin per customer. You can take this margin and see if it is enough to cover the other costs of servicing the customer.

If you take the margin dollars (revenue less any cost of goods), then subtract all the direct expenses relating to that customer, you will get a final profit number for the life of the customer.

Cost to serve analysis

	Customer 1	**Customer 2**
Revenue	$50,000	$3,000
Margin Dollars	**$25,000**	**$1,250**
Shipping Costs	$3,500	$750
Order Entry	$0 (Online)	$25 (Phone Orders)
Order Fulfilment	$50	$20
Customer Service	$20	$200
Accounts Receivable	$0	$100
Profit	**$21,430**	**$155**
Profit Margin	**43%**	**5%**

In this example, Customer 1 is a healthy customer, giving us 43% profit on their orders at a much higher value. Customer 2 is unhealthy, giving us just 5% profit; plus, they never pay on time so we're carrying the cost of their purchase. Keep in mind that these numbers don't include all your OPEX related to the business, so you are still relying on having a healthy profit margin to cover those. In this scenario, you need to deal with customer 2 to resolve this issue long term.

MEDIATION

If you're dealing with another business, they will likely understand that profit is vital to success. Often you can call them and have a candid discussion to see if perhaps they would be willing to order more, or maybe you can address the underlying reason why they need so much customer service. It is ultimately a harmless conversation that may allow you to reduce the cost to serve the customer.

FIRING CUSTOMERS

In the worst-case scenario in which mediation fails, you may need to fire the client. This is never an easy conversation to have but it is necessary to cut the fat. Typically, a politely worded email is all it takes. There are two ways to approach this.

1. Be direct and let them know they're being fired.

This can be worded in a similar way as this example:

"We have recently conducted an annual review of our operations to ensure we are running as efficiently as possible.

As part of this review, we have had to make some difficult decisions regarding our client list. Unfortunately, our current business model can no longer support accounts with [insert reason objectively: e.g., order volumes below $5k/custom labelling requirements /non-standard shipping terms].

Regrettably, this means we will be unable to continue supplying [client company name], effective from [date]."

This ensures the firing is not personal and is just business related.

2. Increase their pricing

This can be worded in a similar way as this example:

"I'm writing to let you know about some changes to our service terms, effective [date].

Due to rising operational expenses, we are updating our wholesale structure. Moving forward, the following changes will apply to your account:

- Minimum Order Quantity: Increased to [amount].
- Service Fee: A surcharge of [amount] will apply to [specific annoying behaviour, e.g., urgent processing/custom packing].

-   Pricing: A [X]% increase across the range."

This approach means technically you're not firing them — you're just adjusting your requirements for them. This ensures that if they continue to be a customer, they at least should return a higher profit margin for you.

In an ideal world, you will never have to fire a client. In the real world, though, you might need to prevent customers from killing your profitability. It may seem counterintuitive to turn away revenue, but as discussed throughout this book, our goal is profit, not just turnover.

MANAGING CASH FLOW

When you give out terms to customers, you are delaying when you get paid, which makes managing cash flow more difficult. It is, however, a part of operations when dealing business to business, so you need to ensure you stay on top of it.

If you are a small business, try to avoid giving out long payment terms unless it is strategic. Start with around 7 days as a default, because it is relatively low risk. If you find a customer is a bad payer, then move them to pre-paid terms, where they have to pay before you ship the order. Medium and large businesses generally have better supplier terms and more stable cash flow, so you can offer more generous payment terms.

Large retailers will often request much longer payment terms like 30, 60 or even 90 days. The advantage of these retailers is they will typically move large volumes of your product. The challenge for you is that you're usually funding the stock well beyond the time it takes to sell through in store. Before you start to accept deals like this, you need to make sure you have capacity, cash flow and the appropriate supplier terms to handle it.

Let's use a 30-day account as an example. If you have 30-day payment terms with your supplier, but stock sits in your warehouse for 60 days before it goes to your customer, then the customer has 30 days to pay you. You have to cover that cost for 60 days between when you've paid the supplier and when the customer pays you.

Cash gap timeline

Day 1	You receive stock
Day 30	You pay the supplier
Day 60	You ship to the customer
Day 90	The customer pays

Sixty days is a long time to be funding stock for, and often you're doing it for your largest customers. You can reduce this time, however, by having more frequent stock turns. For example, if you ship the stock within 7 days of it landing in the warehouse instead of 60 days, your cash gap will only be 7 days. In reality, this is risky and difficult to achieve. Make sure you're aware of your cash gap so you can minimise it wherever possible.

If you're unable to reduce the cash gap by increasing stock turns, or reduce your customers payment terms, you may consider invoice funding. Invoice funding allows you to get paid by a third party for an invoice upfront, long before the customer actually pays. While this is helpful and improves cashflow, it comes at a cost. These services will take a percentage of the invoice eating into your margin. If you are opting to use a service like this, make sure you have the margins to cover it.

CHAPTER REVISION

- Do you have any customers who have a high cost to serve and are ultimately unprofitable for you?
- Do you need to fire any customers?
- What are the shortest payment terms you can produce for customers without throwing away business?
- If you provide long payment terms, what is the cash gap?
- How can you minimise and fund the cash gap?

CHAPTER 9

MARKETING EFFICIENCY OVER MARKETING MAGIC: MASTERING YOUR MARKETING

I'm not going to talk about how to do marketing – that is not really my skillset. It also evolves so fast that it would be out of date before this even goes to print. Instead, we will look at marketing purely from a "sh!t in the middle" perspective – how to understand and measure it, to make sure it is performing for you without sinking your profits.

MARKETING TYPES

There are two main types of marketing: brand marketing and performance marketing. You should be cautious about what advertising you choose to do, because it is easy to lose a lot of money quickly.

BRAND MARKETING

Brand marketing is activity that is designed to generate brand awareness. It doesn't necessarily have a direct return on investment (ROI) and is often measured by eyeballs rather than anything tangible. The goal is for as many people to see the ad as possible and become "aware" of the brand. These are things like billboards, TV, radio, PR, team sponsorship and other out-of-home marketing.

Many small businesses will invest in brand marketing to try to look like a big global brand. The problem is, they don't have the revenue yet to really cover this investment without getting a direct return. Unless you have money to burn, brand marketing should be avoided for small businesses.

PERFORMANCE MARKETING

Performance marketing, on the other hand, is marketing designed to create a conversion or sale. This is highly measurable, because often it is digital and you can track exactly who has clicked on your website and bought from you. The goal of performance marketing is to move customers through the funnel from awareness to purchase. This typically includes social media, Google, email and retargeting. The advertising channels you choose depend on your industry and target audience.

While performance marketing is highly measurable, that is only useful if you are monitoring it regularly and ensuring your ads are high-performing. One of the key ways to measure this is using return on ad spend (ROAS), which we will touch on a bit later.

THE FUNNEL

If you've ever spoken to a marketer, you've probably heard them mention the marketing funnel. In simple terms, it is a way to segment and understand where a customer is within the context of your business. With the tools available today, you can target specific segments of the audience and show them the most relevant ads for their understanding of the brand. The idea is to funnel your targets from the top, all the way through to the bottom of the funnel, where they purchase from you.

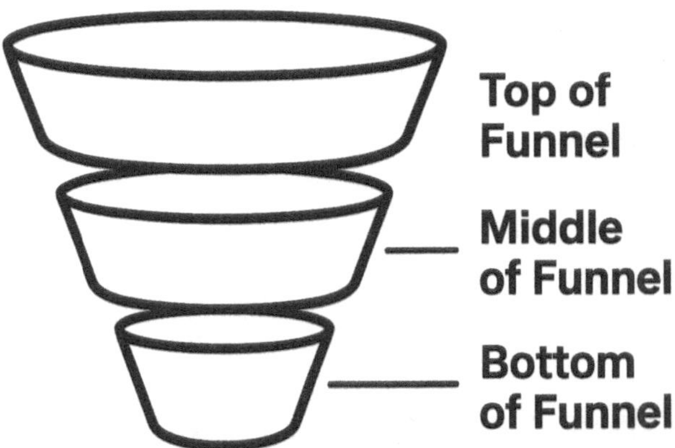

TOP OF FUNNEL

These are customers who have had no interaction with your business at all. This will be the largest portion of customers. When targeting this segment, your conversion rate will generally be lower than other segments because the customer will need more convincing. You can't avoid this segment, however, because the middle and bottom pools are much smaller, and you need to get more top of funnel customers to move down the funnel. These ads are mostly about educating the customer about your product and raising awareness.

MIDDLE OF FUNNEL

These are customers who already know about your brand but have not yet purchased from you. The goal when targeting these customers is to get them to buy. They are aware of your brand, they have seen your ads or perhaps even looked at your website, and they have put something in the cart before abandoning the process. The ads you target this customer with move from awareness ads in the top of funnel, to buy and offer type ads to get them to purchase from you.

BOTTOM OF FUNNEL

These are customers who already know your brand and have purchased from you. You will continue to target this customer to try to get them to buy again and increase their lifetime value. If you release new or limited-edition products, this segment is primed and ready to purchase them. Based on this concept, you will want to retarget them with fresh ads and products.

MEASURING YOUR RETURN, CONTROLLING YOUR SPEND

Now that you understand the basics of marketing, let's get into the juicy stuff. It's not enough to simply create the ads and let them run – you need to monitor them weekly or even daily to ensure they are working for you. With the modern consumer, ads age really fast, so an ad that worked last week might not work this week.

RETURN ON AD SPEND

The main way we measure performance for an ad or ad campaign is via ROAS. This is simply how much money you're getting back for every dollar you're spending on the ad. Less than 1x ROAS and you're losing money, 1x and you're breaking even (on revenue) and 5x you're probably making money.

$$ROAS = \frac{AdRevenue}{AdSpend}$$

The ROAS number you need depends on your margin. If you have a low margin, you require a larger ROAS to ensure you're profitable. If you have a high margin, you can get away with a lower ROAS. It is important to note that the ROAS is looking purely at your revenue, so you're actually making a loss at 1x ROAS because you're not covering your cost of goods and OPEX. You should cut ads that are performing this badly. On the other hand, if you have a high margin product with a 5x ROAS, you can increase the spend on these ads to try to capture more sales.

RETURN ON INVESTMENT

If you're using a marketing agency or consultant, then ROAS is not the right measurement to use. Instead, you need to use ROI, because you're not paying just for ads, you're also paying for the additional fees for the service provided. It is not enough to cover the cost of the ads alone; you need to cover all costs related to the marketing. ROI factors in all the costs to acquire the customer, not just the ad spend. To achieve this, you have to add the additional service fees to the ad costs.

$$ROI = \frac{AdRevenue}{AdSpend + ServiceFees}$$

With these extra costs, it is a lot harder to cover the costs of your marketing. Many small businesses try marketing agencies before their ad spend and return is high enough to do so. When you add this extra cost, you still need to achieve a high ROI to cover the rest of your OPEX and cost of goods. This means your ROAS will have to be much higher than if you managed it internally to start with. When your business grows and has a large investment capacity, then you will be able to more easily cover the service fees of a third party to manage the ads for you.

MARKETING EFFICIENCY RATIO

ROAS or ROI alone will not ensure your marketing is under control. There is another important metric called marketing efficiency ratio (MER). This is simply a measure of how much you are spending relative to your total revenue, usually as a percentage.

$$MER = \frac{Marketing Spend}{Revenue} * 100$$

Which MER works for you depends on your margin and expenses. If you have a high margin, you may be able to get away with a MER as high as 30%. A more typical MER is around 10%. Whatever you decide to go for in terms of MER, you need to factor this into your expenses in the profitability calculations and forecasts we did earlier to ensure it makes sense for your business.

AVERAGE ORDER VALUE

Understanding your average order value (AOV), also referred to as average transaction value is crucial. A low AOV may be the cause of low ROI or MER. The AOV is very straightforward to measure. Simply divide the total value of all your orders by the total number of orders.

$$AOV = \frac{TotalOrderValue}{TotalOrderCount}$$

You always want to achieve the highest possible AOV as you can. There are many ways to increase it – for example, via upsells, increasing free shipping thresholds, gifts with purchases over a certain amount, and many more. What AOV you need is dictated by how much it costs to acquire a customer. Getting your ads to convert is only half the battle, the other half is maximising how much you can get the customer to spend.

CUSTOMER ACQUISITION COST

Another important metric to monitor is your customer acquisition cost (CAC), also referred to as cost per acquisition. This is simply how much it costs on average to acquire a customer. To calculate your CAC, divide the total marketing spend plus any service fees, by the total number of orders.

$$CAC = \frac{AdSpend + ServiceFees}{TotalOrderCount}$$

Unlike ROI and ROAS which measure the return on your spend, CAC simply identifies how much you need to spend to acquire a new customer. If it costs you $100 to acquire a new customer but your AOV is only $50, you need to make sure the lifetime value of your customers is high enough to cover it over the long run.

Performance marketing is not easy. You have a lot of variables, a lot of measures to track, and it is not just set and forget. You need to be specific about where you market, how the ads are presented and worded, and change them out as soon as they stop performing. Measure the performance closely for every channel you have, and make sure the metrics make sense. If a channel doesn't perform for you after trying various campaigns, don't be afraid to drop it. There are a lot of options out there for where to market, so don't get hung up on those that don't work for you.

CHAPTER REVISION

- What is the difference between brand and performance marketing?
- What are the different parts of the marketing funnel?
- What is the ROAS for your ads and campaigns?
- If you're using an agency or consultant, what is the ROI for your campaigns?
- What is your MER, and how does this affect your forecasts?
- What is your current AOV and are there ways you can increase it?
- What is your current CAC?

CHAPTER 10

BALANCE THE LINE: OPTIMISING YOUR OUTPUT

If you produce or manufacture products, you need to think about every process in your production line and how to make it more efficient.

You should think of your manufacturing line as a constantly evolving beast. You should be optimising it all the time, whether it's modifying a process to get you back a few minutes here and there or changing a recipe to make it flow better through the machines. Every minute you gain in production increases your output and saves you money at the same time.

LEVEL THE WORKLOAD

If you've ever watched how car manufacturers produce the volume they do, it is truly fascinating. You have a piece of machinery with tens of thousands of components being meticulously put together every few minutes.

So how do they do this? They break down every task in such a way that each takes the same amount of time. Every car can then move freely from station to station in perfect harmony. At your work station, you will have a specific set of tasks, and those tasks should take an exact amount of time, down to the second. So, every station must complete the task in the specified amount of time. Behind each of the stations are teams working to build or compile the components ready for the next station. That means they have to have, for example, a body, a dashboard, all the doors, etc., all ready in the same amount of time. It is a stunning ballet that is the pinnacle of manufacturing.

What is powerful about this is that the time spent at every station isn't made up according to the tasks but according to demand. There is no point producing a car every 90 seconds if you only sell three a day. Conversely, if you sell a car every 90 seconds, and you can only produce one every 10 minutes, your backlog will get out of control. Car manufacturers finely tune the flow according to demand and they are ruthless about dropping cars that don't sell well for this exact reason. If you have a line that can produce 100,000 cars a year, and you can only sell 20,000 cars, you have a real problem. Carmakers will drop cars that are still selling in the tens of thousands if they are not achieving the optimal output.

While we don't all have the budgets of these massive car manufacturers, we can use their philosophy to improve our production flow. There are a few things that make this flow work really well.

Repetition

Because the team member only works at one station, they complete the same task over and over. This means they know the precise steps to follow each time and can do it on autopilot without making costly mistakes.

Process optimisation

Because of the timing, each process is optimised to ensure the right tools are always ready, the appropriate machinery is used to prevent repetitive strain injuries and all the components are ready to go. You can also identify and remove unnecessary actions promptly, because each step is well thought out with clear purpose.

Training

Each team member is thoroughly trained on their specific process. This ensures the task is completed correctly every time in the right amount of time. Importantly, because a team member is assigned to a specific station, they don't need to learn the requirements of the other stations. They can simply focus on their specific task.

Removing bottlenecks

Because each station has the same amount of work and time in which to complete it, there are no bottlenecks. The work never piles up at a single station and causes later stations to stand around and twiddle their thumbs. If you can make 1,000 chocolate bars per day, but can only pack 500 per day, packaging is creating a bottleneck. To solve this problem, you need to find a way to double the packaging capacity so it is balanced with how many chocolate bars can be produced.

Eliminating downtime

Each station is optimised to remove downtime. Similar to what we discussed in the capacity chapter, you are using the 450 minutes of that team member to get the maximum output without burnout. At the scale of global car manufacturers, extra seconds cost literally tens of thousands of dollars. While it might not be quite to the same scale for your business, it still costs money over time.

BATCH FLOW VS ONE-PIECE

When you first start your business, you'll likely use a batch flow. A batch flow is when you complete each task in batches. For example, you make 1,000 chocolate bars, then wrap all 1,000, then box all 1,000. This seems efficient as you get in a rhythm for each task and is a common way of working.

One-piece flow, on the other hand, is when you complete each task for a single unit before moving onto the next one. For example, you make one bar, then wrap it, box it and repeat. This is the same flow car manufacturers use. In fact, it is also the flow used by large manufacturers around the world. This is because using a one-piece flow is almost always faster and more efficient.

There is logic behind this. With batch flow, you're often waiting for the 1,000 items to finish before the next stage can commence. With a one-piece flow, you can commence the second stage immediately after the first item has gone through the first stage.

There are many other benefits too. You get faster quality feedback, so if the first item has an issue down the line, you can catch it early and course correct. It can require less space because the product moves from start to finish through the line. You also don't need to store 1,000 unfinished products throughout the line.

A one-piece flow doesn't work for all products, of course. Using the chocolate example, if it is handmade it takes a few hours to set after being moulded before it can be bagged. This can be solved by end-to-end automation, but that is not feasible for small businesses. You can, however, consider doing smaller batches to get closer to a one-piece flow. Instead of doing 1,000 bars at a time, do 100. This way, the first batch is ready earlier for the team to pick up and complete the latter stages. Then, for packaging you can adopt the one-piece flow for wrapping and boxing.

AUTOMATE OR DIE

This is one of the oldest sayings out there, and it definitely still holds true today. With the cost of employing staff growing each year, every new person you employ is a compounding cost. This doesn't mean you should not hire humans at all, it simply means use humans for what only humans can do.

When founding the chocolate business, we built the model around handmade. I thought our high margin would drive profitability, but I was wrong. Handmade meant that 70% of the cost of producing an item was labour, and that cost went up every year, and only got worse as we scaled.

If I were to have my time again, I would consider automation from the beginning. With automation, I could have made a consistent, high-quality product without the cost of additional skilled chocolatiers. But the reality is when you first start a business, you can't start with a fully automated line, because you don't have the volume to move the product. So how do you get there?

You start handmade or contract manufactured, and you automate components as you grow and scale. To achieve that, though, you need to know the requirements of a fully or semi-automated line so you can craft a product suitable for it. The work you've done in the previous chapters will be beneficial here. Do your research before you're ready, so when you're ready you can build in the automation in your forecast. You need to understand when it makes sense to automate segments of your line, based on volume and capacity constraints. Also consider if adding the automation will create bottlenecks down the line, and whether there is a way you can deal with them to ensure you get the maximum benefit.

Here's a free tip for you – automation is not cheap, easy or quick. Machines take a long time to configure and get right. Don't expect to buy a piece of equipment and have it fully working on day one. We invested in a flow wrapper; you load the chocolates on a conveyor and they are individually wrapped. It's a very common piece of machinery used in the chocolate industry. It took almost a month to get the machine set up properly to work with our specific wrap and chocolates. More complicated lines can take longer, so work that into your plans.

Of course, you can always use a contract manufacturer to get you going. They will likely have a lot of the automation already in their lines. They will also require minimum quantities to make it work and have certain constraints. The benefit of a contract manufacturer is that they already have the volume to cover the fixed overheads that you would otherwise be funding if you had your own facility. So even though you're going to be giving them extra margin, it is only relative to the amount you order, so the risk is much lower. Again, the work you've done in earlier chapters will help you find the right contract manufacturer for the volumes you need.

REDUCING WASTAGE

Wastage is effectively throwing away revenue. Whether it be from wastage due to the process and mistakes or wastage due to quality issues, it all costs money. Its source can come from anywhere – for example, a bad component from a supplier or an ineffective process.

When you've created your recipe, you will likely have an idea of what the ingredient wastage is. But you need to track what the actual wastage is on a consistent basis. The best way to do that is to follow the expected yield versus actual yield. Earlier in the book we talked about tracking every production run – this is precisely what we're doing here. If you find that every batch or lot you are producing is falling short of the expected yield, something is wrong. This is when you need to investigate the root cause. Is it a process not being followed? Is it a changed ingredient that is affecting your output? Is it a bad process that must be fixed? Whatever it is, you need to understand it and resolve it. If you produce $1,000,000 worth of product a year, a 1% variance in the output is worth $10,000 each year.

When reviewing your processes, remember: once is a mistake, multiple times is a process issue. When you see a pattern, automate or simplify the step to ensure it never happens again.

To enforce these processes at scale, larger businesses will generally introduce a Quality and Safety Manager who is responsible for maintaining the quality and safety of every item produced. Depending on the industry, there are typically standards and certifications to follow. For example, in the food industry there are HACCP, SQF and many other standards. These require certain levels of documentation that can bog down production. But if you implement these processes correctly (with the right tools) you will likely also reduce wastage. Your processes will be stronger, which in turn will reduce the chances of a production issue or recall. Time spent here will save you money in the long run.

PRODUCING THE RIGHT AMOUNT

Every unit you overproduce is cash you can't use elsewhere. That money sits on a shelf gathering dust instead of growing your business. For perishable goods, it's even worse – that capital has an expiration date, and once it passes, you've literally thrown profit in the bin.

When working out what to produce and when, your forecast is your friend yet again. It helps give you an idea of how much to produce and when, because you have already worked out how many units you need. Once you've got sales data, you can use both your forecast and your weeks on hand report to work out the right amount to produce.

The goal is to never be out of stock, but also, never have too much stock. The best way to work this out is to understand how frequently you can produce this item and how long it takes. If the item takes 2 days to produce, and you can make it every week, then you simply produce how much you require for the following week with a 10% cover if needed. Follow it closely with your weeks on hand so you don't overproduce.

Where it gets trickier is when you have a long lead time, like 6 months. It's extremely difficult to predict what sales will be in 6 months' time. You don't have the ability to make more quickly if it goes well, and if it goes poorly, then you've got one hell of a problem. Using your forecast and weeks on hand reports here will help you predict what you need to produce. But at this range, data only gets you so far. You need a contingency plan. If stock moves slowly, how will you clear it? If you have reliable clearance channels, it is safer to overproduce than underproduce. Use your best-case forecast as your target but treat that as a hard ceiling – producing beyond it is just gambling.

CHAPTER REVISION

- How can you level the workload across stations within your production facility?
- Can you introduce more repetitive tasks, to make them more efficient?
- Are there any bottlenecks that need to be dealt with to improve efficiency?
- Are there unnecessary processes that can be removed?
- Are there any processes that you can automate in your business to improve efficiency?
- Is there unnecessary wastage in your recipes?
- Is the actual yield you're getting consistent with your expected yield?
- How much do you need to produce and when to ensure you're not over or underproducing?

CHAPTER 11

STOP FLYING BLIND: DATA IS YOUR BEST FRIEND

I've seen far too many business owners who run their business blind. No forecasting, no inventory levels, and even some who don't know how to read a P&L. If this is you now, ask yourself, would you drive a car blind? The reality is you wouldn't. So why are you running your business that way? Data is your friend.

The problem seems to stem from two main sources. The first is a lack of time to get a proper system up and running. You're pushing a cart with square wheels and don't want to stop for a moment to put on round wheels.

The second is a lack of money – or perceived lack of money. All businesses are spending money. Whether it's rent, utilities, salaries or ingredients, there is a big chunk of money going out. Technology that delivers data is just another cost on a big pile of other costs. The point they're missing is that data is what they need to break the cycle. They need the ability to see exactly what things cost, to understand if they're on track to reach profitability.

TECHNOLOGY FOR DATA

Stop flying blind. Invest in the right tools to get you the data you need to make better decisions. The challenge is, there are countless systems out there, many that talk a big game but in reality don't deliver. I built Supply'd ERP specifically to solve the problems in this book, but these principles apply whether you use software or a spreadsheet. I'll dive into how to pick the right software for you a bit later on.

When I say data, I'm not just talking about revenue and sales. You can get that from most software. Instead, you want to be able to deep dive and, more importantly, have a single source of truth. A source of truth is a place where you can look at the data and know it is accurate. You can have other systems connected to it, like your point of sale, ecommerce site, or accounting software. And just to be clear – your accounting software is rarely a good source of truth.

So, what makes a good source of truth? Usually, it's a system that has all of your sales, operational and purchasing data, as well as inventory. Typically, your accounting software misses the operational context, meaning at least 25% of your critical data is missing. Occasionally, you can bridge the gap with business intelligence software, but finding dedicated operational software is far easier.

Once you have the software, be sure to check it regularly. Stay on top of sales, purchasing, inventory and margins so that you know where you stand at any given time.

TECHNOLOGY FOR OPERATIONS

Many ERP software packages out there focus mostly on accounting. They have really in-depth accounting capability but lack the tools you need for operations. This is where you want to instead look for an operating system, operational ERP or warehouse management system because this is where you will get the most benefit from an investment standpoint. The more tools you can find in the one piece of software, the better. Just do your due diligence to ensure that they are full-featured and not half-cocked.

One of the key strategies we have with Supply'd ERP is to use PDA scanners for warehouse and floor staff so they can do more of their job in situ rather than needing to jump on a computer. The team can use a scanner to receive stock, instantly put stock into the system, pick and pack and stocktake. This makes the team much more efficient and, honestly, it makes the job more fun.

A good piece of operational software will take the tasks you do today and make them more efficient. Some tasks may take the same amount of time but give you the benefit of more data so that you can continue to optimise your operations and get gains elsewhere.

When looking for an operating system for your business, you should consider the full scope of what's required. Often, businesses will look at problems in isolation – for example, a piece of software to track production. This leads to a narrow focus and disparity across the business. You should instead map out all the different parts of your business, and the requirements for each one – everything from point of sale and production to pick and pack, deliveries and accounting. While it may not be feasible to get a system that does all areas well, you may be able to find a system that does most of it well and integrates nicely with tools you already have. If all areas are mapped out, you will better understand the big picture and how they all talk to one another.

AVOID SILOS

A common issue with choosing software is the danger of silos. The finance team has certain requirements so they go off and find something that suits them. That software doesn't support the warehouse, so now you plug in a warehouse management system. Now, your sales channels are not centralised so you add an order management system. Your drivers need the deliveries routed so they go and get a transport management system. The sales team need a place for their customers so they choose a customer relationship manager. Before long, you have every team working in different systems with siloed views of the business.

The danger here is that all teams are working in isolation. The warehouse team can't see the pipeline coming through from the customer relationship manager, the transport team are unsure of the orders to be fulfilled until their picked. Ultimately this leads to a lot of manual communication. Instead, zoom out and bring the team together to scope the wholistic requirements. Obviously, this will take more time – perhaps time that the teams think they don't have. But it is just a cart with square wheels scenario all over again. Take the time to do the work upfront and save all the needless communication and divide that is caused from disparate systems. I've seen this firsthand too many times, particularly in medium-to-large enterprises.

Small businesses have a unique advantage: As the owner, you are the ultimate "silo-breaker" because you're across every department. But that advantage only works if you map your requirements from end-to-end before buying into the next shiny software tool. Even if you can't afford the all-in-one solution today, having a map ensures you aren't building a tech stack that requires a team of humans to bridge the gaps with manual data entry. Stop building on disparate systems and start implementing a single source of truth.

FIND THE RIGHT SOFTWARE FOR YOU

Not all tools are right for all businesses. We've tailored Supply'd ERP to the food and retail sector. We don't really work with fashion brands, for example. So, when you're looking for software, you need to try to look for something built for your industry rather than something generic. Generic might be okay if you have simple needs, but many industries need something more tailored.

There are so many different pieces of software out there, it can be hard to find what you need. Try to be as specific as you can when searching or asking AI for the solution you need. Often, the first page, and first AI recommendations, will be the large, well-known players. Be sure to dig deeper, search the second and third pages, and challenge the AI to give you more suitable recommendations. Even if AI is aware of a better solution, it might not share it with you initially, particularly if it is an up-and-coming brand. Software comparison sites can be helpful to locate lesser-known competitors for what you need. They will also commonly feature reviews, which may be able to help guide you on the suitability and ease-of-use. Keep in mind though, many of these sites charge the software companies to be featured near the top. Because of this, the niche software you need might be buried further down the list, after all the known brands.

When you think you have found the right software, you will want to do your due diligence before going ahead. Don't get fooled by flashy PowerPoint presentations and slick salespeople. Always do a demo, have a set of requirements written down and ask them to cover the "how" of each of them. It is one thing to say it can do something – often the "how" is where things can come unstuck. Salespeople will always sell the destination, they rarely show you how to get there. I've worked with clients who had a 30-step process on multiple legacy systems that was reduced to a 7-step process using a modern solution without silos. It united teams while saving tens of thousands of minutes per year.

Demo at least three different pieces of software so you get an idea of the pros and cons of each. All software is different and some will have features others don't, so having a list of needs is useful to check off what is available in each. Keep in mind, the good software companies are constantly evolving, so there may be software that ticks off 80% of what you require today, but within 6 months it might cover off the remaining 20% for you – it's just about going on the journey.

Another thing to check is how exportable the data is. Some software providers will try to lock down your data so you can only access it within their software. Remember this is your data not theirs, so you should be able to freely export it at any time without needing to contact support.

This brings me to my last point – try to find software with a decent free trial period. This allows you to get your hands dirty with the software, but more importantly, get a feel for the support provided by the software provider. ERP and inventory software are challenging to implement so your processes may need to adjust to suit the software you're using. The free trial is your opportunity to play around but also ask plenty of questions. Once you give the go ahead, you'll be more comfortable that the software suits you and that the support you need is there.

LICENSING AND CONSULTING

Beware of the licensing and consulting trap. There is a lot of software out there for which you need to pay first a licensing fee, then a consultancy fee to customise the solution for you. This is fine for large businesses with money to burn, but small and medium businesses should avoid this option unless they have extremely specific requirements not covered by out-of-the-box solutions. The trap here is that you will be quoted for the licensing of the ERP software, which is all well and good, but then you will get a quote from your consultancy on the changes required. I have heard many horror stories of a product being quoted at $25,000 but ending up costing more than $300,000 over the course of 3 years due to countless unknowns by either party or scope creep. Unfortunately, once you start, it's extremely hard to turn back. So, your consultant can give a low quote knowing you're locked in after you pay the first bill with no choice but to keep paying through the teeth; otherwise, you'll throw away tens of thousands of dollars.

However, there are scenarios in which it is useful to have consultants, like when you need help implementing the software. Just make sure the scope is well defined and clear for both parties. Usually, the cost blowouts come from software customisations that may already be available in an off-the-shelf solution. If your consultant is steering you towards a customised solution, tread carefully. It would be worth doing some more research yourself to make sure they're not guiding you based on what is best for themselves.

CHAPTER REVISION

- What are all the processes in the business that could benefit from technology?
- What software options are available for your industry to give you the data you need to grow?
- What are the best software tools for your business?
- What improvements will the software deliver for your business processes?
- Is there software that will unite all your teams into a single source of truth?
- What data will you have that you currently do not use, and how will you use that data to optimise the business?
- Do you need a consultant, or can you do the research yourself?

SUMMARY

The sh!t in the middle is arguably one of the hardest things to control. As you will have read in this book, there are countless moving parts that require constant iteration and monitoring to ensure you're not throwing money away.

When cash flow is tight, you need to go back to square one and get the basics right. Often, that is where you'll uncover the root cause of the problem. Most businesses chase the top line by pouring money into marketing or expanding headcount, only to find their expenses growing even faster than their revenue. This is like trying to fill a bucket with a massive hole in the bottom. By instead mastering the sh!t in the middle, you finesse your expenses so they grow at a slower rate than your sales. This is how you stop pouring effort into a leaky bucket and finally start building real, sustainable profit.

NOW, GO DO THE WORK

As mentioned multiple times in this book, you need to be consistent. Starting today, and then every day moving forward, try to optimise something in your business. Check your performance against your forecast and make sure you're on track for profit. Make sure your team is not burning out and implement the right tools to ensure you are running as efficiently as possible.

The best businesses don't necessarily have the best product, but they do show up every day with a plan. They recognise that a great product is a starting point, but a sound strategy and a clear path to profitability are what keep the business alive. If your operations are leaking cash, throwing money at marketing won't save you. But if you follow the frameworks in this book and commit to optimising the sh!t in the middle every day, you'll find that profitability isn't a mystery – it's the result of replacing the square wheels with round ones.

THE SH!T IN THE MIDDLE MANIFESTO

Revenue is vanity.
We do not celebrate top line growth if the bottom line is slimmer than a gluten-free pancake.

Respect the sh!t in the middle.
Expenses often grow as fast as revenue. If you ignore them, they will kill your business.

Forecasts are maps, not guesses.
We plan for the best-, the realistic, and the worst-case scenarios so we are never surprised.

Humans are not robots.
A human has 3 to 4 hours of critical thinking a day. Find ways to reduce the critical thinking required in each task.

Automate or die.
If a machine can do it, a machine *should* do it. Save your humans for what only humans can do.

Stock is cash.
Inventory is just money sitting on a shelf that you can't spend. Holding too much is as dangerous as having too little.

Fire bad customers.
Not all revenue is good revenue. If the cost to serve a customer destroys the margin, fire them.

Wastage is lost revenue.
Every 1% of yield you lose in production is money you literally threw in the bin. Fix the process.

Data beats gut feel.
Stop driving the car blind. If you don't have a single source of truth, you don't have a business – you have a hobby.

Do the work.
There is no silver bullet. Focus on continuous optimisation of all processes in your business.

YOUR NEXT READ

Mastering the sh!t in the middle gives you the foundation, but a great business requires a constant appetite for learning. These are the books that helped me navigate the rest of the journey:

- The No Bullsh!t Strategy by Alex H Smith
- Profit First by Mike Michalowicz
- Rework by Jason Fried and David Heinemeier Hansson
- The Goal by Eliyahu Goldratt
- Never Split the Difference by Chris Voss

THE TERMINOLOGY

Often in business, many specific terms and acronyms are used. This makes it difficult to get up to speed with what experienced businesspeople are saying. To assist you, here is a comprehensive list of abbreviations and their meaning.

Business terms

Term	Meaning
Business to Business (B2B)	Selling from one business to another
Business to Consumer (B2C)	Selling from your business direct to consumers
Consumer Packaged Goods (CPG)	Items packaged to sell to consumers
Cost to Serve	The total cost to your business to service a specific customer
Direct to Consumer (D2C)	Selling from your business direct to consumers
Fast Moving Consumer Goods (FMCG)	High-volume and fast-selling consumer packaged items
Last Mile	The last vehicle or method used to deliver the item to the customer
Oddment	An odd size or colour of an item that is not yet sold
Rate of Sale (ROS)	How many units of an item you're selling on average each day (or week/month)
Sales Channel	The channel through which you sell a product (e.g. online, retail, wholesale)
Source of Truth	A single piece of software or document that has accurate data and reporting for all business functions

Stock Available	How much stock you have available to sell (the amount on hand less any stock reserved for orders)
Stock on Hand	How much stock you physically have in your warehouse(s)
Stock Turn	How many times a year your stock turns over
Unique Selling Point (USP)	The unique feature or function of your business or product that makes customers buy you over your competitors
Wholesale	Selling direct to a retailer or manufacturer

Accounting terms

Term	Meaning
Bottom Line	Your Net Profit
Cash Gap	The gap between when you have to pay for stock and when the customer pays for it
Cost of Goods Sold (COGS)	The cost of items you have sold
Earnings Before Interest and Tax (EBIT)	Your earnings before interest and tax
Earnings Before Interest, Tax, and Amortisation (EBITA)	Your earnings before interest, tax, and amortisation
Earnings Before Interest, Tax, Depreciation, and Amortisation (EBITDA)	Your earnings before interest, tax, depreciation, and amortisation
End of month (EOM)	Usually prefixed with the number of days after the end of the month that an invoice is due
End of week (EOW)	Usually prefixed with the number of days after the end of the week that an invoice is due
Gross Profit	How much profit you have BEFORE any operating expenses
Landed Costs	The final cost of an item with all freight and duty charges factored in
Margin	How much gross profit you make per sale

Net Profit	How much profit you made after all expenses
Operating Expenses (OPEX)	Any expenses that are related to operating the business
Payment Terms	How long you have to pay invoices
Profit & Loss (P&L)	A statement showing your revenue, expenses and resulting profit or loss
Revenue	Total sales
The Sh!t In The Middle	Operations and expenses
Top Line	How much revenue you've made

Software and Hardware terms

Term	Meaning
Business Intelligence (BI)	Reporting software to view aggregated data dashboards and reports
Customer Relationship Manager (CRM)	Sales and customer management software
Enterprise Resource Planning (ERP)	Software to centralise your data into a single source of truth
Inventory Management System (IMS)	Software to keep track of your inventory
Manufacturing Resource Planning (MRP)	Software to manage your manufacturing and production
Order Management System (OMS)	Software to aggregate your orders
Personal Digital Assistant (PDA)	A handheld device similar to a mobile phone, designed to assist workers
Product Information Management (PIM)	Software to manage your product library
Transport Management System (TMS)	Software to manage your deliveries and vehicles
Warehouse Management System (WMS)	Software to manage your warehouse

Marketing terms

Term	Meaning
Average Order Value (AOV)	The average value of each order
Average Transaction Value (ATV)	The average value of each transaction
Click-Through Rate (CTR)	How many people click on an ad, relative to how many saw the ad
Cost Per Acquisition (CPA)	How much it costs to acquire a customer
Cost Per Impression (CPI)	Cost per ad view (usually per 1,000 views)
Customer Acquisition Cost (CAC)	How much it costs to acquire a customer
Email Direct Marketing (EDM)	Sending email marketing to a mailing list
Lifetime Value (LTV)	The lifetime value of a customer
Marketing Efficiency Ratio (MER)	What percentage of revenue was spent of marketing
Out-of-Home (OOH)	Out-of-home marketing such as billboards and radio ads
Retargeting	Targeting ads to customers who have already shown interest or visited your site
Return on Ad Spend (ROAS)	How many times the ad spend was returned from revenue
Return on Investment (ROI)	How many times the total investment was returned from revenue

ACKNOWLEDGMENTS

All the knowledge instilled in this book wouldn't be possible without those who I've shared my journey with across the years.

Thank you to my wife, Anya. I couldn't imagine anyone better to share my business journey with. You are truly one of a kind, hard-working, always pushing yourself and those around you to make things better. You balance me out, and I don't think I would have been able to write this book without you in my corner.

To my family, especially my parents Kim and Wayne. You taught me wrong from right, and you supported me through the times when money was tight. Although I am the forgotten middle child, you were always there when I needed you, so thank you!

To those who helped me along my business journey – Pancho Gutstein, Sean Smith, Michael Cusack and Boyd Roberts. You each provided me guidance and feedback that I still remember and use to this day. Whether it's strategy, forecasting or pushing me to be better, your support helped shape a lot of the thoughts in this book.

Thank you to all my Supply'd teammates, investors, partners and clients. You are the group of people who I have perhaps learned the most from in business. There are too many of you to name individually, and the list is growing all the time – you know who you are. The candid discussions we have around business, ideas, inspiration and challenges help me grow every day.

To my copy editor, Tina Morganella, thank you for your efforts to help educate me on how to write better and polish the words. Being my first book, I've really just been fumbling through it. To my book designer, Karolina Kruk-Umięcka, thank you for bringing to life the visual side of this book. I didn't want to have a boring novel, so your work on making that a reality is appreciated!

Last but not least, thank you to you. Yes, you. I had a lot of thoughts I wanted to get onto paper, and I'm so happy you've taken the time to read them, and even read the acknowledgments. That is commitment, and it is appreciated!

ABOUT THE AUTHOR

Jason Stockton is the founder of Supply'd ERP, which is an operational platform designed to help food and retail businesses scale through precision and efficiency. With a foundation in software engineering, Jason has spent his career bridging the gap between complex technology and real-world business results.

His journey into "the sh!t in the middle" was forged in the trenches. Notably, Jason founded a handcrafted chocolate business in Australia — which he successfully sold in 2024 — after learning firsthand that even the world's best product can't survive without sound unit economics. Prior to his entrepreneurial ventures, he served as the ecommerce manager for PUMA Oceania, where he oversaw massive digital growth and navigated the operational chaos of three major warehouse moves.

Today, Jason uses those "hard way" lessons to help other founders stop flying blind and start building businesses that are as profitable as they are productive.